HELOC Risk Management

How to Use Home Equity Without Over-Leveraging or Losing Your Home

By Joseph G. Correa

Licensed Mortgage Broker, Finibi Mortgage

Copyright & Legal Notice

First Edition, 2026

Table of Contents

Foreword

The reason this book exists is simple: home equity is one of the most powerful financial tools ever created for ordinary people. Over the last several decades I have watched families change their lives by tapping into their equity wisely, and I have also watched people lose everything because they treated their home like an ATM instead of a financial engine. Book 9 of *The Home Equity Wealth Series* is the pivot point of the entire collection because this is where empowerment meets responsibility. Up to this point you have learned how HELOCs work, how to qualify, how to use them to invest, eliminate debt, and build wealth, but none of that matters if you do not understand how to protect yourself from risk. This book exists to make sure the tool that can build your future never becomes the reason you lose it.

In today's world, homeowners are constantly being pushed to borrow more. Ads promise easy approvals, fast cash, and instant access to tens or hundreds of thousands of dollars. Banks and fintech companies market HELOCs as if they are just another credit card, but they are not. A HELOC is secured by your home, which means the stakes are higher, the rules are different, and the consequences are real. That does not mean HELOCs are dangerous, it means they must be used with a level of strategy and discipline that most people are never taught. The goal of this book is not to scare you away from leverage, but to give you a professional framework so you can use it confidently, intelligently, and safely.

As a licensed mortgage broker working with homeowners, real estate investors, and business owners every day, I see the same mistakes repeated over and over. People overestimate how much equity they should use, underestimate how quickly balances can grow, and fail to plan for changing interest rates, income disruptions, or market downturns. The tragedy is that most of these outcomes are preventable with the right structure. This book teaches you how to think like a financial professional instead of a borrower. You will learn how to evaluate risk before you pull a single dollar, how to build safety buffers into your HELOC strategy, and how to make sure your home remains a shield instead of a liability.

One of the biggest myths in personal finance is that all debt is bad. The truth is that unmanaged debt is bad, but structured leverage is how real wealth is built. Every major real estate portfolio, business empire, and investment fund in the world uses borrowed money, but they do so with strict rules, ratios, and exit plans. Homeowners are rarely given access to those same frameworks, which is why so many people either avoid leverage entirely or use it recklessly. This book bridges that gap. It gives you the same thinking used by professional investors and lenders, translated into clear, practical steps you can apply to your own home equity.

Risk management is not about avoiding action, it is about controlling outcomes. When you use a HELOC with the right structure, you are not gambling with your home, you are putting your equity to work in a way that is measured, protected, and reversible. You will learn how to calculate safe utilization levels, how to stress-test your finances against rate increases or income changes, and how to design exit strategies before you ever deploy capital. These are the habits that separate borrowers who thrive from borrowers who panic when conditions change.

This book is especially important in an economy where interest rates, home values, and lending standards can shift quickly. What works in a rising market can become dangerous in a flat or declining one if you are not prepared. That does not mean you should sit on the sidelines. It means you should move forward with a playbook that anticipates change instead of reacting to it. HELOC risk management is not about predicting the future, it is about building flexibility into your financial life so no matter what happens, you remain in control.

You will also discover that risk is not just financial, it is psychological. Easy access to large sums of money changes behavior. Without clear rules, people overspend, chase bad investments, or turn short-term opportunities into long-term burdens. This book helps you create personal guardrails so you never use your HELOC out of emotion, pressure, or impulse. Instead, every dollar you deploy will have a purpose, a return expectation, and a clear path back to zero.

Book 9 sits at the heart of *The Home Equity Wealth Series* because it protects everything you are building. Books 1 through 8 show you what is possible with home equity. This book ensures you keep it. And Book 10 will show you how to integrate all of it into a lifelong blueprint for financial independence. When you master HELOC risk management, you are no longer a homeowner hoping things work out. You become a strategist who understands leverage, controls exposure, and uses their home as a true financial asset.

My goal in writing this series has always been to give homeowners the same clarity and confidence that professionals have. Your home is likely your largest asset. It deserves more than guesswork and marketing slogans. It deserves a plan. This foreword marks the beginning of the most important conversation you will have about your equity, not how much you can use, but how to use it without ever putting what matters most at risk.

Chapter 1

Understanding Risk Before You Borrow

Before you ever draw a single dollar from a HELOC, the most important question you must answer is not how much you can borrow, but how much you should borrow. Risk in home equity lending does not come from the loan itself, it comes from how it interacts with your income, your cash flow, your lifestyle, and your future. A HELOC is a powerful financial tool precisely because it is flexible, but that same flexibility can create danger if it is not guided by structure. This chapter establishes the foundation for everything that follows by teaching you how to think about risk the way lenders, investors, and financial institutions do, instead of the way consumers are taught to think about credit.

The first concept you must understand is that your home is not just a place to live, it is a balance sheet. Every property has a value, a debt position, and an equity position. When you open a HELOC, you are converting a portion of your equity into usable capital. That capital is not free money, it is borrowed money secured by the most important asset you own. The risk is not that you borrow, the risk is that you borrow without a clear plan for repayment, income replacement, or asset growth. Every responsible use of home equity starts with defining the role that borrowed money will play in your financial life.

One of the most common mistakes homeowners make is focusing only on their credit limit. If a bank offers a $200,000 HELOC, many people assume that means it is safe to use $200,000. In reality, the credit limit is not a recommendation, it is simply the maximum exposure the lender is willing to take. Safe borrowing is based on cash flow, not just collateral. You must always ask how much of that balance you can carry without stress if interest rates rise, income drops, or the investment you are funding takes longer than expected to pay off.

This leads to the most important rule of risk management: your HELOC must be supported by cash flow, not hope. Whether you are using your HELOC to pay off debt, invest in real estate, start a business, or build passive income, there must be a realistic path that replaces or exceeds the monthly payment you are creating. If your HELOC increases your required monthly payments by $1,000, your plan must reliably generate at least $1,000 in additional cash flow or savings. Anything less means you are slowly tightening financial pressure instead of creating freedom.

Interest rate risk is another factor most borrowers ignore. HELOCs are typically variable-rate loans, which means the payment can increase even if your balance does not. A line that costs $800 per month today could cost $1,100 per month a year from now. Proper risk management means stress-testing your numbers before you borrow. You should calculate what your payment would be if rates rise by two, three, or even four percent and make sure you can still comfortably afford it. If you cannot, the balance you plan to carry is too high.

Another overlooked risk is liquidity. When you move money from your home into an investment or business, you are trading a highly liquid asset, equity, for something that may be difficult to convert back to cash quickly. If an emergency happens and you need to reduce your HELOC balance, you must have access to cash or sellable assets. This is why professionals never deploy all available capital. They always keep reserves. Your HELOC strategy should include a cash buffer equal to several months of payments and living expenses so you are never forced to sell or borrow in a crisis.

There is also behavioral risk. Easy access to large sums of money changes how people think. Without rules, a HELOC can turn into lifestyle inflation instead of wealth creation. That is why you must define, in writing, what your HELOC is for and what it is not for. Risk-managed HELOCs are used for debt reduction, income-producing assets, and strategic investments. They are not used for vacations, cars, shopping, or anything that does not increase financial stability or earning power.

The final risk to understand is exit risk. Every use of leverage should have an exit plan. That means knowing how and when you will pay the HELOC down or off entirely. Some exits come from refinancing, some from selling assets, some from rental income, and some from business cash flow. What matters is that you do not enter a leverage position without a clear, realistic way out. A HELOC without an exit plan is not a strategy, it is a gamble.

When you understand these risks, HELOCs stop being scary and start becoming powerful. You are no longer borrowing blindly. You are deploying capital with intent, protection, and foresight. The rest of this book builds on this foundation, showing you exactly how to use these principles in real-world scenarios so your home equity works for you without ever putting your home in danger.

Practical Example: *Applying Risk Management With Real Numbers*

Let's look at a homeowner named Sarah who owns a home valued at $500,000. She owes $250,000 on her first mortgage. That means she has $250,000 in equity. A lender offers her a HELOC up to 80 percent of her home's value. Eighty percent of $500,000 is $400,000. Since she already owes $250,000, the maximum possible HELOC would be $150,000. That is the credit limit, but it is not the amount she should use.

Sarah earns $8,000 per month after taxes. Her existing mortgage payment, including taxes and insurance, is $2,000. Her other monthly living expenses total $3,000. That means she has $3,000 per month in surplus cash flow before any HELOC payments. If she took the full $150,000 HELOC at a 9 percent interest rate, her interest-only payment would be about $1,125 per month. That fits within her $3,000 surplus, but risk management means looking further.

Sarah stress-tests the payment at a 12 percent interest rate. At 12 percent, the same $150,000 would cost about $1,500 per month. That leaves her with $1,500 in remaining surplus. That still works, but now she must consider what she is using the money for. Sarah plans to use the HELOC to buy a rental property that will generate $1,800 per month in net cash flow after expenses. If that income is reliable, it covers even the higher interest payment and still leaves her positive.

Now Sarah looks at liquidity. She does not want to deploy all $150,000. Instead, she decides to use only $120,000 for the investment and keep $30,000 in her HELOC unused as an emergency buffer. That means her actual payment at 9 percent is $900 per month and at 12 percent is $1,200 per month. With rental income of $1,800, she still clears $600 even in a higher-rate scenario.

Next, Sarah defines her exit plan. She plans to either refinance the rental property into a long-term loan or sell it within three to five years. If she refinances, the new loan will pay off the $120,000 HELOC balance. If she sells, she will use the sale proceeds to clear the HELOC. In both cases, the HELOC is not permanent debt, it is temporary capital.

Now Sarah calculates her total exposure. She has a $250,000 first mortgage and plans to use $120,000 of her HELOC, for a total of $370,000 in debt on a $500,000 home. That is 74 percent loan-to-value, which is below the 80 percent maximum and gives her a $130,000 equity cushion. Even if home values drop by 10 percent, her home would still be worth $450,000, leaving her $80,000 in equity.

When Sarah compares this to someone who maxes out the full $150,000 HELOC with no cash reserves and no income plan, the difference is clear. Sarah has cash flow coverage, interest rate protection, liquidity, and an exit. The other borrower only has hope. This is what risk-managed HELOC use looks like. Every number supports the strategy, every dollar has a purpose, and every risk has a buffer.

This is how home equity becomes a tool for wealth instead of a threat to your future.

Chapter 2

Setting Safe Borrowing Limits

One of the most dangerous misconceptions about HELOCs is that the bank's approval amount equals a safe amount to use. In reality, lenders approve based on collateral and broad underwriting rules, not on how resilient your personal finances are under stress. Safe borrowing limits are something you must define yourself. This chapter teaches you how to create your own borrowing ceiling that protects your home, your cash flow, and your long-term financial stability regardless of what a lender offers.

The foundation of safe borrowing starts with understanding that your HELOC is not meant to replace your income, it is meant to amplify it. Any amount you borrow must be serviceable by your current or future cash flow without creating anxiety or forcing lifestyle changes. That means the true borrowing limit is not based on your equity alone, but on how much monthly payment your budget can absorb under worst-case conditions. This is the same way banks think when they evaluate large commercial loans, and it is the same way you must think as a homeowner using leverage. To determine your personal safe borrowing limit, you begin with your free cash flow. Free cash flow is the money left over each month after you pay all of your required living expenses, your mortgage, insurance, food, transportation, and any existing debt. This number represents your true capacity to service new debt. A conservative risk management rule is that no more than 50 percent of your free cash flow should be used for HELOC payments. The other 50 percent remains as protection against income changes, emergencies, and rate increases.

The next step is to account for interest rate risk. HELOCs are variable, so you never calculate payments at today's rate alone. You must also calculate what your payment would be if rates rise by at least three percent. If your HELOC payment would still fit comfortably within your 50 percent free cash flow limit at that higher rate, the balance is within your safe zone. If not, the borrowing amount must be reduced until it fits.

Another critical factor is your total loan-to-value ratio. Even if your cash flow supports a large HELOC, you should never allow your total mortgage debt to rise above a level that puts your home at risk in a market downturn. A professional rule of thumb is to keep your combined loan-to-value at or below 75 percent whenever possible. That means at least 25 percent of your home's value remains as a buffer against falling prices, refinancing problems, or unexpected life events. Liquidity is also part of your borrowing limit. You should never deploy every dollar of your HELOC. At least 20 percent of your available line should remain unused as a financial safety valve. This protects you if an investment takes longer than expected, a tenant stops paying, or a business experiences slow months. Liquidity is what allows you to survive stress without selling assets or making desperate decisions.

Your safe borrowing limit is therefore determined by four factors working together: free cash flow, stress-tested interest rates, loan-to-value ratios, and liquidity reserves. When all four align, you have a borrowing amount that is not just approved, but sustainable. This is the difference between leveraging your home and gambling with it.

Once you establish your personal borrowing limit, you must treat it as a hard rule. It does not matter if home values rise or the bank increases your credit line. Your safe limit only changes when your income increases, your debts decrease, or your overall financial position improves. This discipline is what allows you to use home equity repeatedly over a lifetime without ever putting yourself in a fragile position.

When you approach HELOCs this way, borrowing becomes boring, predictable, and safe. That is exactly what you want. The goal is not excitement, it is stability with upside. A HELOC used within safe limits becomes a wealth-building engine that quietly works in the background while your life moves forward.

Practical Example: *Calculating a Safe Borrowing Limit*

Let's look at a homeowner named Mark. Mark owns a home worth $600,000. His current mortgage balance is $300,000. That means he has $300,000 in equity. A bank offers him a HELOC up to 80 percent of the home's value. Eighty percent of $600,000 is $480,000. Since he owes $300,000, the maximum possible HELOC is $180,000. That is the bank's limit, but Mark is about to calculate his own.

Mark's monthly income after taxes is $9,000. His mortgage payment is $2,200. His other living expenses, including food, utilities, insurance, car payments, and subscriptions, total $3,800. That means his free cash flow is $9,000 minus $6,000, which equals $3,000 per month. According to the 50 percent rule, Mark should use no more than $1,500 of that for HELOC payments.

Mark checks current HELOC rates and sees they are 9 percent. At 9 percent, a $100,000 HELOC would have an interest-only payment of about $750 per month. A $150,000 HELOC would cost about $1,125 per month. Both fit under his $1,500 limit at today's rate. But Mark must stress-test.

Mark increases the rate by 3 percent to 12 percent. At 12 percent, a $100,000 HELOC would cost about $1,000 per month. A $150,000 HELOC would cost about $1,500 per month. That means $150,000 would max out his safe payment limit under a higher-rate scenario, leaving him with no buffer. $100,000 would leave him $500 of protection. From a cash flow standpoint, $100,000 is safer.

Now Mark checks his loan-to-value ratio. If he borrows $100,000, his total debt becomes $400,000. Divided by his $600,000 home value, that is 66 percent loan-to-value. That is well below the 75 percent safety threshold. If he borrowed $150,000, his total debt would be $450,000, which is 75 percent loan-to-value. That is still acceptable, but right at the upper limit. The $100,000 option gives him more equity protection.

Next Mark considers liquidity. The bank offered him $180,000. If he only uses $100,000, he keeps $80,000 unused as a reserve. That is more than 40 percent of the line, which gives him a strong safety net. If he used $150,000, he would only have $30,000 unused, which is much tighter.

When Mark looks at all four factors together, the math points to a $100,000 HELOC as his safe borrowing limit. Even though the bank offered $180,000, his personal risk-managed limit is $100,000. That amount fits his cash flow even if rates rise, keeps his loan-to-value conservative, and leaves him with strong liquidity. This is how professional-level risk management works. You do not ask how much you can borrow, you calculate how much you should borrow. By doing this, Mark can confidently use his HELOC to invest, eliminate debt, or grow income without ever putting his home or his lifestyle in danger.

Chapter 3

Cash Flow as Your Primary Safety Net

When most homeowners think about risk with a HELOC, they think about their home value. In reality, the true protection of your home is not equity, it is cash flow. Cash flow is what allows you to make payments when markets change, interest rates rise, or investments take longer than expected to perform. If your HELOC strategy is built on strong cash flow, your equity remains protected. If it is built on appreciation or optimism, even a small disruption can create stress. This chapter explains why cash flow is the foundation of safe leverage and how to structure your HELOC so it is always supported by income.

Cash flow is simply the difference between what you earn and what you spend each month. When you add a HELOC to your financial picture, you are adding a new obligation. That obligation must be covered not just today, but in the future under different conditions. That is why professional investors never rely on best-case projections. They plan for average and worst-case scenarios. Your HELOC should be able to survive months where income dips, expenses rise, or returns come in lower than expected. The first step is to calculate your baseline cash flow without any HELOC. This means subtracting all required expenses from your net income. Required expenses include your mortgage, taxes, insurance, utilities, food, transportation, and minimum debt payments. What remains is your free cash flow. That number is the raw fuel that supports any leverage you take on. A HELOC payment should never exceed a portion of that free cash flow. If it does, you are building a fragile structure.

The second step is to calculate your HELOC payment not just at today's rate, but at a higher stress-tested rate. If your HELOC rate is 8 percent, you should also calculate it at 11 or 12 percent. This shows you what your payment could become. Your cash flow must be able to cover that higher payment comfortably. If it cannot, the HELOC balance you plan to carry is too high, even if the bank approved it.

Next, you must look at how the money you borrow affects your cash flow. If you use your HELOC to pay off credit cards or personal loans, you may actually improve cash flow by replacing high-interest payments with lower ones. If you use it to invest, the investment should produce income that replaces or exceeds the HELOC payment. Every use of home equity should either increase cash flow or reduce financial pressure. If it does neither, it is not a safe use of leverage.

Cash flow also provides psychological safety. When you know your HELOC payment is covered by real income, you do not panic when rates move or headlines change. This allows you to think long-term instead of reacting emotionally. Panic is what causes people to sell assets at the wrong time or make bad financial decisions. Cash flow gives you patience.

Another important concept is margin. Margin is the amount of cash flow left after all payments are made. If your HELOC payment is $1,000 and you only have $1,050 of free cash flow, you are operating with a $50 margin. That is dangerous. A safe HELOC strategy maintains a margin of at least several hundred dollars per month, and ideally much more. This margin absorbs unexpected expenses and protects you from stress.

Finally, you must remember that cash flow is not static. Jobs change, businesses have slow months, tenants move, and expenses rise. That is why you never structure a HELOC at the maximum your current cash flow allows. You always leave room for life. This is what separates sustainable leverage from reckless borrowing.

When cash flow is the center of your HELOC strategy, risk becomes manageable. Your home is protected not by hope, but by numbers. This allows you to use leverage confidently to build wealth without sacrificing stability.

Practical Example: *Using Cash Flow to Protect a HELOC*

Let's look at a homeowner named Daniel. Daniel earns $7,500 per month after taxes. His mortgage payment is $1,900. His other required expenses, including food, utilities, car, insurance, and debt payments, total $3,100. That means his total required expenses are $5,000. Subtracting that from his $7,500 income leaves him with $2,500 in free cash flow.

Daniel owns a home worth $450,000 and owes $230,000. A lender offers him a HELOC of $130,000. Daniel wants to use $100,000 of it to invest in a small rental property. At a 9 percent interest rate, a $100,000 HELOC has an interest-only payment of about $750 per month. Subtracting that from his $2,500 free cash flow leaves him with $1,750 of margin. That looks safe, but Daniel must stress-test.

Daniel increases the rate to 12 percent. At 12 percent, the $100,000 HELOC would cost about $1,000 per month. Now his margin becomes $2,500 minus $1,000, which equals $1,500. That is still strong. Even if his income dropped by $500 one month, he would still be able to make the payment without stress.

Now Daniel looks at the rental income. The property he is buying is expected to generate $1,400 per month in net cash flow after expenses. That means the rental more than covers the $1,000 stress-tested HELOC payment, leaving $400 extra. This turns the HELOC into a self-sustaining investment instead of a burden on his personal income.

Daniel now checks his total debt. His first mortgage is $230,000. His HELOC will be $100,000. That means total debt is $330,000. Dividing that by his $450,000 home value gives a loan-to-value of about 73 percent. That leaves him with 27 percent equity as a buffer, which is within safe risk-managed guidelines.

If Daniel had borrowed the full $130,000, his payment at 12 percent would be about $1,300 per month. His rental would only cover $1,400, leaving him with $100. That tiny margin would mean any vacancy, repair, or rate increase would push him into stress. By choosing $100,000 instead of $130,000, Daniel created safety.

This is how cash flow protects your home. The numbers work together. The income covers the debt, the margin absorbs surprises, and the equity buffer protects against market changes. Daniel is not guessing. He is managing risk with math.

Chapter 4

Interest Rate Risk and How to Neutralize It

One of the most misunderstood risks in HELOCs is not the balance, but the interest rate. Because most HELOCs are variable, the amount you owe can stay the same while your payment quietly rises. Many homeowners focus only on how much they borrowed and ignore how sensitive their payment is to rate changes. This chapter shows you how interest rate risk works, why it matters more than most people realize, and how to design your HELOC strategy so rate increases never threaten your home or your peace of mind.

A variable interest rate means your HELOC payment is tied to a benchmark, usually the prime rate plus a margin. When the Federal Reserve raises rates, your HELOC rate rises. That means your monthly interest cost increases even if you do not borrow another dollar. If you are carrying a large balance, a small change in rates can add hundreds or even thousands of dollars to your monthly payment. The danger is not that rates move, it is that borrowers are unprepared for them to move.

The first rule of interest rate risk management is to never base your strategy on today's rate. You must always assume that rates will eventually rise. The question is not if, but how much. A conservative planning assumption is to stress-test your HELOC payment at least three percent higher than your starting rate. If you can afford the payment at that higher rate without strain, you have built a buffer against volatility.

The second rule is to keep balances lower than the maximum you qualify for. High balances magnify the impact of rate increases. For example, a two percent rate increase on a $50,000 balance is far less painful than the same increase on a $150,000 balance. By keeping your borrowed amount within safe limits, you reduce how sensitive your finances are to rate changes.

Another powerful way to manage interest rate risk is to match variable-rate debt with income that grows or adjusts over time. If you use your HELOC to buy a rental property, rents can rise over time. If you use it to grow a business, revenue can increase. This natural growth can offset higher interest costs. This is why productive uses of HELOCs are safer than consumption.

Some lenders also offer fixed-rate conversion options within a HELOC. This allows you to lock in a portion of your balance at a fixed rate for a set period. While fixed rates are often higher than variable rates at the start, they provide certainty.

Strategic borrowers sometimes fix part of their balance to reduce exposure while leaving another part variable to take advantage of lower rates.

Timing is also a form of risk management. Drawing large balances when rates are already high leaves less room for them to rise further, while borrowing aggressively when rates are low can expose you to large increases later. This does not mean you should try to time the market, but it does mean you should be extra conservative when rates are unusually low.

Finally, interest rate risk is managed by having a plan to reduce or eliminate your HELOC balance over time. The less you owe, the less rate changes matter. Even if you use interest-only payments initially, you should always have a long-term plan to pay the line down through refinancing, asset sales, or cash flow from investments.

When you design your HELOC strategy with interest rate risk in mind, you stop being vulnerable to forces you cannot control. Rates can rise or fall, but your plan remains stable. This is how professionals use variable-rate leverage without fear.

Practical Example: *Stress-Testing a HELOC Against Rate Changes*

Let's look at a homeowner named Lisa. Lisa has a home worth $520,000 and a first mortgage of $260,000. She opens a HELOC with a limit of $150,000. Lisa plans to use $120,000 of it to renovate and rent out a duplex. Her HELOC rate starts at 8.5 percent.

At 8.5 percent, the interest-only payment on $120,000 is about $850 per month. Lisa's free cash flow before the HELOC is $2,400 per month, so after the HELOC payment she would have $1,550 left. That feels comfortable, but Lisa must plan for higher rates.

Lisa increases the rate by three percent to 11.5 percent. At 11.5 percent, the payment on $120,000 becomes about $1,150 per month. Now her remaining cash flow is $2,400 minus $1,150, which equals $1,250. That is still safe, but she looks deeper.

Lisa also increases the rate to 13.5 percent as an extreme case. At 13.5 percent, the payment is about $1,350 per month. That leaves her with $1,050 of margin. That is still workable, but she wants additional protection.

The duplex she is renovating will generate $1,600 per month in net cash flow after expenses. That income will cover even the $1,350 worst-case HELOC payment and leave her $250 extra. That means the HELOC is self-supporting even if rates rise sharply.

Lisa also decides not to use the full $150,000 line. By only using $120,000, she leaves $30,000 unused. That means if the renovation goes over budget or rents come in late, she has a buffer without needing to borrow elsewhere.

Now Lisa checks her loan-to-value. Her total debt will be $260,000 plus $120,000, which equals $380,000. Divided by her $520,000 home value, that is about 73 percent. That gives her a 27 percent equity cushion.

When Lisa looks at the numbers, she sees that even under higher rates, her HELOC payment is covered by rental income, supported by her personal cash flow, and backed by equity and liquidity. That is how interest rate risk is neutralized. The numbers are not fragile. They are layered with protection.

Chapter 5

Liquidity, Reserves, and Why Access to Cash Protects Your Home

One of the most common ways homeowners get into trouble with a HELOC is not because they borrowed too much, but because they left themselves with no room to breathe. Liquidity is the ability to access cash when you need it. Reserves are the cash or unused credit that you keep available for emergencies, surprises, and opportunities. Together, they are what keep a smart HELOC strategy from turning into a crisis. This chapter explains why liquidity matters more than most people realize and how to structure your home equity so it always works for you instead of trapping you.

When you use a HELOC, you are turning equity into debt. That debt must be paid regardless of what happens in your life or the economy. If your income drops, a tenant moves out, a business has a slow month, or a major expense shows up, you still owe the HELOC payment. Liquidity is what allows you to handle those situations without stress. Without liquidity, even a small disruption can force you to miss payments, sell assets at the wrong time, or make emotional financial decisions. The first principle of liquidity management is that you should never deploy all of your HELOC. A HELOC is not just a loan, it is a financial safety net. At least 20 percent of your available line should remain unused at all times. That unused portion is what you draw from if a project goes over budget, income is delayed, or an unexpected expense appears. When you use the entire line, you have no backup.

The second principle is cash reserves. In addition to unused HELOC capacity, you should also keep actual cash in the bank. A professional standard is three to six months of required expenses and HELOC payments combined. This cash buffer allows you to survive disruptions without touching your investments or running up other high-interest debt. It turns uncertainty into a manageable inconvenience instead of a financial emergency.

Liquidity also gives you negotiating power. If you have cash or available credit, you can take advantage of opportunities when they appear. You can make repairs, cover vacancies, or even invest when others are forced to sell. Without liquidity, you are always reacting instead of acting.

Another important concept is that not all assets are liquid. Money tied up in real estate, businesses, or long-term investments cannot always be accessed quickly without losses. That is why you must not confuse net worth with liquidity. You can be wealthy on paper and still be cash-poor. A safe HELOC strategy ensures that you always have some capital that can be used immediately.

Reserves also protect you psychologically. Knowing that you have money available reduces stress and prevents panic. This allows you to make rational decisions instead of emotional ones. Panic is what destroys wealth. Liquidity is what preserves it.

Finally, liquidity is what allows you to hold your investments long enough for them to succeed. Many good deals fail not because they were bad, but because the investor ran out of cash before they paid off. By maintaining reserves, you give your investments time to mature and your strategy time to work.

When liquidity and reserves are built into your HELOC plan, risk becomes manageable. You are no longer walking a financial tightrope. You are standing on solid ground with room to move.

Practical Example: *How Liquidity Prevents Financial Stress*

Let's look at a homeowner named Carlos. Carlos has a home worth $480,000 and a first mortgage of $240,000. He opens a HELOC with a limit of $140,000. Carlos wants to use his HELOC to buy and renovate a rental property that will eventually generate income. Carlos earns $8,000 per month after taxes. His required expenses, including his mortgage, are $5,200 per month. That means he has $2,800 in free cash flow. He plans to use $100,000 of his HELOC. At a 9 percent interest rate, the interest-only payment is about $750 per month. That leaves him with $2,050 of monthly margin.

Instead of using the full $140,000, Carlos leaves $40,000 unused. That is about 29 percent of his line, which exceeds the 20 percent reserve rule. This $40,000 is his emergency liquidity. If the renovation goes over budget or a tenant moves out, he can access this money without applying for another loan.

Carlos also keeps $20,000 in a savings account. His total required monthly expenses including the HELOC payment are now $5,950. Three months of that would be about $17,850, so his $20,000 cash reserve meets the three-month guideline.

During the renovation, Carlos runs into a $15,000 unexpected plumbing and electrical issue. Instead of panicking, he draws $15,000 from his unused HELOC capacity. His total HELOC balance becomes $115,000. At 9 percent, the payment becomes about $860 per month. His free cash flow is still $2,800 minus $860, which equals $1,940. He is still safe.

If Carlos had used the full $140,000 from the start, he would have had no unused credit. He would have had to use credit cards or delay the project, which could have cost him much more. Because he kept liquidity, the surprise became manageable.

When the rental is finished, it produces $1,500 per month in net cash flow. That covers the $860 HELOC payment and leaves $640 extra. Carlos uses that $640 to rebuild his cash savings and gradually pay down the HELOC. Over time, his balance decreases, his risk falls, and his financial position strengthens.

This is how liquidity protects your home. It turns uncertainty into a minor inconvenience instead of a disaster.

Chapter 6

Exit Strategies and How to Get Out Cleanly

The most overlooked part of any HELOC plan is not how you get in, but how you get out. Every use of borrowed money should have a clear, realistic exit strategy before the first dollar is spent. An exit strategy is simply the plan for how and when the HELOC balance will be reduced or paid off. Without an exit, even a profitable investment can turn into long-term risk. This chapter teaches you how to design exits that protect your home, lock in gains, and keep leverage working in your favor.

An exit strategy does not mean you intend to fail. It means you intend to finish. Professionals never enter a leveraged position without knowing how they will unwind it. This could mean refinancing, selling an asset, using cash flow to pay down the balance, or rolling the debt into longer-term financing. What matters is that the HELOC is temporary capital, not permanent debt.

The first rule of exit planning is that the HELOC should never be the final resting place for long-term debt. HELOCs are variable-rate, short-term tools. Long-term assets like rental properties, businesses, or large projects should eventually be moved into fixed-rate or amortized loans when appropriate. This protects you from interest rate risk and frees your HELOC for future opportunities.

The second rule is that your exit must be based on realistic numbers, not optimistic projections. If you plan to sell a property, you must account for selling costs, taxes, and market fluctuations. If you plan to refinance, you must assume conservative property values and interest rates. Your exit should still work even if conditions are not perfect.

Cash flow exits are another powerful option. This means using the income from the investment funded by the HELOC to gradually pay the line down. This reduces risk over time and increases your equity. Even small monthly principal payments can dramatically improve your long-term safety.

You should also have a backup exit. If your primary plan fails, there should be a secondary way to reduce the balance. This might include selling another asset, using savings, or downsizing. A HELOC backed by multiple exits is far safer than one with only a single plan.

Timing is part of exit planning. You should define a target date by which the HELOC balance will be significantly reduced or eliminated. This prevents the line from quietly becoming permanent debt. Deadlines create discipline.

When exit strategies are built into your HELOC use, leverage becomes a tool instead of a trap. You are no longer hoping things work out. You are planning for them to conclude in your favor.

Practical Example: *Building a Real Exit Strategy*

Let's look at a homeowner named Rebecca. Rebecca owns a home worth $550,000 and owes $280,000. She opens a HELOC with a limit of $160,000 and uses $120,000 to buy a small rental property.

At 9 percent, her HELOC payment is about $900 per month. The rental produces $1,500 per month in net income. That leaves $600 per month after the HELOC payment.

Rebecca decides her primary exit strategy is refinancing the rental into a long-term mortgage in three years. She expects the rental to be worth $200,000 after renovations. If she refinances at 75 percent loan-to-value, she could get a loan of $150,000. That would be enough to pay off the $120,000 HELOC and leave $30,000 for closing costs and reserves.

Rebecca also calculates a cash flow exit. If she uses the extra $600 per month to pay down the HELOC, that is $7,200 per year. Over three years, that is $21,600. That would reduce her HELOC balance from $120,000 to about $98,400, making refinancing even easier.

Rebecca also identifies a backup exit. She has $40,000 in savings and a brokerage account she could tap if needed. This means she is not dependent on a single outcome.

When Rebecca combines these numbers, she sees that even if the rental value only reaches $180,000, 75 percent of that is $135,000, which would still be enough to clear a $98,400 HELOC. Her exits overlap and reinforce each other.

This is what a clean exit looks like. The HELOC is not a permanent burden. It is a temporary bridge to a stronger financial position.

Chapter 7

Psychological Risk, Discipline, and Avoiding HELOC Traps

The final layer of HELOC risk management has nothing to do with interest rates, loan-to-value ratios, or spreadsheets. It has everything to do with human behavior. The biggest danger to your home is not the loan, it is the decisions you make once you have access to large amounts of money. Easy access to equity changes how people think, spend, and take risks. This chapter teaches you how to build discipline, avoid common psychological traps, and keep your HELOC aligned with your long-term financial goals.

When people receive a large credit line, their perception of money shifts. A balance that once felt expensive suddenly feels distant because it is secured by a home and spread over time. This leads to a false sense of affordability. A $100,000 HELOC does not feel as real as a $100,000 cash withdrawal, even though the obligation is exactly the same. Without strong rules, this mental disconnect leads to overspending and misuse.

One of the most dangerous traps is lifestyle inflation. Homeowners begin using their HELOC for renovations that do not add value, luxury purchases, or expenses that do not generate income. Each draw may seem small, but over time the balance grows and the monthly payment becomes a burden. Risk management means committing in advance that your HELOC is a financial tool, not a lifestyle enhancer.

Another trap is overconfidence. When an investment works, people assume the next one will too. This leads to increasing leverage without increasing safety. Professionals do the opposite. As they grow, they become more conservative with risk. They protect their base while allowing upside. This mindset keeps them in the game long-term.

Discipline also means tracking your numbers. You should know your HELOC balance, interest rate, and payment every month. You should know how much unused credit you have and how much cash you have in reserves. When you monitor these numbers, you catch problems early. When you ignore them, they grow silently.

Rules are what protect you from yourself. These rules include maximum borrowing limits, minimum cash reserves, approved uses for HELOC funds, and required exit plans. When you follow these rules, you remove emotion from your financial decisions. You stop reacting and start executing.

The final psychological risk is procrastination. Many homeowners intend to pay down their HELOC but keep postponing it. Years go by and the line becomes permanent debt. A disciplined plan includes automatic payments, scheduled reviews, and clear milestones for reduction.

When you master the psychology of leverage, HELOCs become a tool of empowerment instead of temptation. You stay in control because your decisions are guided by structure, not emotion.

Practical Example: *Discipline in Action*

Let's look at a homeowner named Brian. Brian has a HELOC with a $120,000 limit and a current balance of $80,000. His payment at 9 percent is about $600 per month. Brian also earns $10,000 per month and has $3,000 in free cash flow.

Brian creates rules. He decides his HELOC can only be used for income-producing investments or debt reduction. He also sets a rule that his balance can never exceed $100,000 and that he must keep at least $20,000 of his line unused.

Brian also sets an automatic principal payment of $500 per month in addition to interest. That means each year he pays down $6,000. If his balance starts at $80,000, after one year it will be $74,000. After two years it will be $68,000.

Brian tracks his numbers monthly. When an opportunity comes up to spend $10,000 on a luxury item, he checks his rules. It would push his balance to $90,000, which is still under his $100,000 limit, but it would not generate income. He declines.

Instead, Brian uses $15,000 to invest in a side business that produces $1,000 per month. That income covers his HELOC payment and his principal reduction, keeping his balance falling instead of rising.

After three years, Brian's balance is around $62,000. His income has grown, his risk has dropped, and his home is safer. That is what discipline looks like in numbers.

Chapter 8

Stress-Testing Your HELOC Strategy Before Life Does It for You

A safe HELOC strategy is not built on what you expect to happen, but on what could happen. Stress-testing is the process of intentionally modeling worse-case scenarios so you can see whether your financial structure can survive them. Professional lenders, hedge funds, and real estate investors all stress-test their deals before committing capital. Homeowners almost never do, which is why so many HELOC plans collapse when conditions change. This chapter teaches you how to pressure-test your numbers so no single event can knock you off balance.

The first principle of stress-testing is to assume that something will go wrong. This is not pessimism, it is realism. Income fluctuates, tenants move out, interest rates rise, and unexpected expenses appear. A HELOC that only works if everything goes perfectly is not a strategy, it is a gamble. A stress-tested HELOC still works when several things go wrong at once.

The starting point is your baseline cash flow. You must know exactly how much you earn, how much you spend, and how much margin you have after all required payments. That margin is what absorbs shocks. If your margin is thin, your structure is fragile. If it is wide, your structure is strong.

Next, you stress-test interest rates. If your HELOC rate is 8 percent today, you calculate payments at 11 percent and 13 percent. This shows you how sensitive your cash flow is to rate increases. Your margin should remain positive even at these higher rates.

Then you stress-test income. If you earn $8,000 per month, you test what happens at $7,000 or $6,500. If you rely on rental income, you assume a vacancy or lower rent. The goal is to see whether your HELOC payment is still covered under reduced income conditions.

You also stress-test expenses. You assume repairs, medical bills, or business slowdowns. This forces you to see whether your reserves and liquidity are sufficient.

Finally, you stress-test asset values. You assume home values drop by 10 or 15 percent. You check whether your loan-to-value ratio remains safe. This protects you from being trapped if refinancing or selling becomes necessary.

When all of these tests are run together, you see the true strength of your HELOC strategy. If it survives, you can move forward with confidence. If it fails, you adjust the numbers before reality does it for you.

Practical Example: *A Full HELOC Stress Test*

Let's look at a homeowner named Olivia. Olivia earns $9,000 per month after taxes. Her required expenses, including her mortgage, total $6,000. That gives her $3,000 in free cash flow. She has a HELOC balance of $110,000 at 8 percent, which costs about $733 per month. That leaves her $2,267 of margin.

Olivia stress-tests the interest rate at 11 percent. At 11 percent, her payment becomes about $1,008. Now her margin is $3,000 minus $1,008, which equals $1,992. She then tests at 13 percent. The payment becomes about $1,192, leaving her $1,808.

Next she stress-tests income. She reduces her income by $1,000 to $8,000. Her free cash flow becomes $2,000. At a 13 percent rate, her margin would be $2,000 minus $1,192, which equals $808. That is still positive.

Then she adds a $500 unexpected expense. Her free cash flow becomes $1,500. After the $1,192 HELOC payment, she still has $308. That is tight, but survivable.

Now she checks asset values. Her home is worth $500,000 and she owes $250,000 on her mortgage. With the $110,000 HELOC, her total debt is $360,000, which is 72 percent loan-to-value. If her home drops by 15 percent to $425,000, her loan-to-value becomes about 85 percent. That is higher, but still not underwater. This tells her she should plan to reduce her HELOC balance over time to lower risk.

Because Olivia stress-tested in advance, she knows exactly how much pressure her finances can handle. She is not guessing. She is managing risk with math and foresight.

Chapter 9

Building a Permanent Risk Management System

The true goal of HELOC risk management is not to survive one deal, one investment, or one financial cycle. The goal is to build a system that protects you for decades. A system is something that works automatically, even when you are busy, distracted, or emotional. Without a system, people start strong but drift into risky behavior over time. This chapter shows you how to turn everything you have learned into a permanent structure that keeps your home safe while allowing your wealth to grow.

A risk management system begins with written rules. These rules define how much you can borrow, how much you must keep in reserves, what you are allowed to use your HELOC for, and how you will exit each use of leverage. When these rules are written down, they become objective. You no longer have to debate with yourself. You simply follow the system.

The next layer is tracking. You should track your HELOC balance, interest rate, payment, free cash flow, reserves, and loan-to-value ratio. This can be done in a simple spreadsheet or notebook. What matters is that you review these numbers at least once per month. This turns your financial life into something you manage, not something that happens to you.

Automation is another critical part of a system. Automatic payments, automatic transfers to savings, and scheduled principal reductions remove procrastination and emotion. If your HELOC is being paid down every month without you having to think about it, your risk decreases steadily over time.

A strong system also includes regular stress tests. At least once per year, you should re-run your numbers assuming higher rates, lower income, and lower property values. This allows you to catch problems early and adjust before they become emergencies.

The final component is growth discipline. As your income and assets increase, your rules should not loosen automatically. In fact, professionals often become more conservative as they become wealthier. They protect what they have built. Your system should evolve, but it should always prioritize stability over maximum leverage.

When risk management becomes a system instead of a one-time decision, you stop worrying about whether your HELOC is safe. It simply is.

Practical Example: *A HELOC Risk System in Action*

Let's look at a homeowner named Natalie. Natalie has a home worth $600,000 and a mortgage of $300,000. She has a HELOC limit of $180,000 and a current balance of $120,000. Her free cash flow is $3,500 per month, and her HELOC payment at 9 percent is about $900.

Natalie's system includes a rule that no more than 50 percent of her free cash flow can go to HELOC payments. Fifty percent of $3,500 is $1,750, so her $900 payment is well within limits. She also has a rule that her loan-to-value must stay below 75 percent. Her total debt is $420,000 on a $600,000 home, which is exactly 70 percent.

Natalie also keeps $25,000 in cash and $60,000 unused in her HELOC. That gives her liquidity equal to more than six months of expenses and payments.

Every month, Natalie pays $900 in interest and an additional $600 toward principal. That means she reduces her balance by $7,200 per year. After one year, her balance falls from $120,000 to $112,800. After three years, it falls to about $98,400.

Natalie also runs a yearly stress test. If her interest rate rises to 12 percent, her payment would be about $1,200. That is still under her $1,750 limit. If her income dropped by $1,000, her free cash flow would be $2,500, and her payment would still be manageable.

Because Natalie follows her system, her risk decreases every year. Her equity grows, her balance shrinks, and her confidence increases. This is what long-term HELOC safety looks like.

Chapter 10

The Professional Home Equity Risk Framework

At this point in the book, you understand every individual piece of HELOC risk management: cash flow, borrowing limits, interest rates, liquidity, exits, psychology, and stress-testing. What remains is learning how to combine all of these into a single professional-grade framework you can use for the rest of your life. This chapter brings everything together into a simple, repeatable system that turns your home equity into a controlled financial engine instead of a source of uncertainty.

The professional framework starts with four pillars: cash flow, equity, liquidity, and exits. Every HELOC decision must satisfy all four. Cash flow means the payment is always covered even under stress. Equity means your total debt stays below a safe percentage of your home's value. Liquidity means you always have access to cash or unused credit. Exits mean you know how the HELOC balance will be reduced or eliminated. If any pillar is weak, the entire structure becomes unstable.

The first step is to define your personal thresholds. This includes the maximum percentage of free cash flow you will allow for HELOC payments, the maximum loan-to-value ratio you will tolerate, the minimum cash and unused credit you will maintain, and the maximum time a balance can remain outstanding. These thresholds turn vague ideas into concrete rules.

The second step is to create a deployment process. Before using your HELOC, you run the numbers through your four pillars. You calculate the payment at higher interest rates, you verify your equity buffer, you confirm your reserves, and you document your exit. This process prevents impulsive decisions and forces discipline.

The third step is ongoing management. Every month, you update your numbers. Every year, you stress-test. As your income and assets grow, you may adjust your limits, but you never abandon the framework. This is what keeps leverage safe over decades instead of months.

The final step is optimization. As HELOC balances decline and equity grows, you can reuse the line for new opportunities. Because you are managing risk instead of ignoring it, your home becomes a renewable financial resource rather than a one-time gamble.

This framework allows you to think like a bank. Banks survive recessions, rate cycles, and market crashes because they operate on systems, not emotions. Now you can do the same.

Practical Example: *Applying the Full Framework*

Let's look at a homeowner named Victor. Victor owns a home worth $700,000 and owes $350,000. He has a HELOC limit of $200,000 and currently uses $140,000. His income after taxes is $11,000 per month, and his required expenses are $7,000. That gives him $4,000 in free cash flow.

Victor's first pillar is cash flow. At a 9 percent rate, his $140,000 HELOC costs about $1,050 per month. At 12 percent, it would cost about $1,400. Victor's rule is that HELOC payments cannot exceed 50 percent of his free cash flow, which is $2,000. Even at the higher rate, his payment is below that.

The second pillar is equity. His total debt is $350,000 plus $140,000, which equals $490,000. Divided by $700,000, that is 70 percent loan-to-value. His maximum allowed is 75 percent, so he is within limits.

The third pillar is liquidity. Victor keeps $30,000 in cash and $60,000 unused in his HELOC. That gives him $90,000 in available reserves.

The fourth pillar is exits. The investment funded by the HELOC generates $2,000 per month. Victor uses $1,000 to cover the HELOC payment and $500 to pay down principal. That is $6,000 per year. In five years, that reduces the balance by $30,000, while he also plans to refinance or sell the asset if needed.

When Victor reviews all four pillars, every one is strong. That means his HELOC is not a risk, it is a tool. This is how professionals use home equity safely and profitably over a lifetime.

Chapter 11

When to Pause, Reduce, or Stop Using Your HELOC

One of the most important skills in risk management is knowing when not to borrow. A HELOC is not something you use continuously without interruption. It is a tool that must be adjusted as your financial life, the economy, and your personal circumstances change. This chapter teaches you how to recognize the warning signs that it is time to pause, slow down, or even reverse your use of home equity so you never cross from strategic leverage into dangerous exposure.

The first category of warning signs comes from your cash flow. If your free cash flow begins to shrink, whether from reduced income, higher expenses, or rising interest rates, your margin of safety decreases. The moment your HELOC payment starts consuming more than the amount you originally planned, it is time to stop drawing on the line and start paying it down. Cash flow is the heartbeat of your financial system. When it weakens, leverage must be reduced.

The second warning sign is declining reserves. If your cash savings or unused HELOC capacity drops below your minimum safety threshold, you are operating without a cushion. This is when small problems become big ones. When reserves fall, new borrowing must stop and rebuilding liquidity becomes the priority.

The third signal comes from the market. If home values begin to fall or lending standards tighten, refinancing and selling become harder. This increases exit risk. In these conditions, the smart move is to reduce balances and protect equity, not to add leverage.

The fourth signal is personal stress. If your HELOC keeps you awake at night, even if the numbers technically work, that is a sign your risk tolerance has been exceeded. Financial strategies must be sustainable emotionally as well as mathematically. Anxiety leads to bad decisions.

The fifth signal is opportunity cost. If better, safer opportunities appear and your HELOC is tied up in low-return uses, it may be time to unwind and reallocate. Leverage should always be working as hard as possible for you.

Learning when to slow down is what separates long-term success from short-term wins. The goal is not to maximize borrowing, it is to maximize longevity.

Practical Example: *Recognizing When to Change Course*

Let's look at a homeowner named Kevin. Kevin earns $8,500 per month after taxes. His required expenses are $5,500, leaving him $3,000 in free cash flow. He has a HELOC balance of $120,000 at 9 percent, which costs about $900 per month. That leaves him $2,100 in margin.

Over time, Kevin's interest rate rises to 12 percent, making his payment about $1,200. His margin drops to $1,800. Then Kevin's company cuts hours, reducing his income to $7,500. His free cash flow becomes $2,000. After the $1,200 HELOC payment, he now has only $800.

Kevin also used some of his reserves to cover business expenses, reducing his savings from $25,000 to $12,000. His safety buffer is shrinking.

When Kevin reviews these numbers, he sees multiple warning signs. His payment now uses 60 percent of his free cash flow instead of the 50 percent he originally allowed. His reserves are below his three-month target. Even though he is not in trouble yet, the trend is negative.

Kevin decides to stop drawing on his HELOC and begins paying down principal by $500 per month. That reduces his balance by $6,000 per year. After one year, his balance drops to $114,000, lowering his payment and rebuilding margin. He also uses part of his income to rebuild his cash savings back to $25,000.

By responding early, Kevin turns a potentially dangerous situation into a manageable adjustment. This is what smart risk management looks like in real life.

Chapter 12

Turning Risk Management Into Long-Term Wealth Protection

The final goal of HELOC risk management is not simply avoiding mistakes, it is creating a financial structure that protects and compounds your wealth for the rest of your life. When risk is controlled, leverage becomes repeatable. When leverage is repeatable, your home becomes a renewable financial engine instead of a one-time opportunity. This chapter shows how disciplined risk management turns short-term borrowing into long-term wealth protection.

The difference between people who build lasting wealth and people who experience financial booms and busts is not intelligence or opportunity, it is survival. Wealth compounds when you stay in the game. Every financial collapse happens when leverage overwhelms stability. HELOC risk management ensures that never happens to you.

When you use home equity within safe limits, supported by cash flow, reserves, and exits, you are no longer exposed to catastrophic failure. You may have setbacks, but you will not be forced out. This is what allows you to reinvest, scale, and benefit from time. Long-term wealth is not built in one deal. It is built by repeating small, safe, profitable uses of leverage over decades. Each time you deploy your HELOC and pay it back, your equity grows. Each time your equity grows, your capacity increases. This creates a compounding loop.

Risk management also protects your family. Your home is more than an asset, it is security. A well-managed HELOC strengthens that security by increasing income, reducing bad debt, and creating financial flexibility. A poorly managed one threatens it. The difference is discipline.

By treating your HELOC like a professional portfolio instead of a personal loan, you give yourself the ability to grow without fear. You are no longer gambling with your future. You are engineering it.

Practical Example: *Compounding Wealth With Safety*

Let's look at a homeowner named Andrea. Andrea owns a home worth $650,000 and owes $325,000. She opens a HELOC and uses $100,000 to invest in income-producing assets.

At 9 percent, her HELOC payment is about $750 per month. The assets generate $1,400 per month, leaving $650. She uses $400 to pay down principal and $250 to increase her savings.

After one year, she has paid down $4,800 of principal. After five years, she has paid down $24,000. Her balance drops to $76,000.

At the same time, her home value rises modestly to $720,000. Her first mortgage is now $310,000 and her HELOC is $76,000. Her total debt is $386,000. Divided by $720,000, her loan-to-value is 54 percent. That means she has built massive safety.

Because her risk is low, Andrea can repeat the process. She uses another $80,000 to fund a new investment, always within her rules. Each cycle increases her income and equity.

This is how HELOC risk management turns into lifelong wealth protection.

Chapter 13

Using HELOCs Safely Across Different Economic Cycles

A truly professional HELOC strategy does not assume the economy will always cooperate. Markets rise, fall, stall, and recover, and your home equity plan must survive all of those phases. Most financial disasters do not come from bad tools, they come from using the right tool at the wrong time without adjusting strategy. This chapter teaches you how to adapt your HELOC use as the economy changes so your home stays protected no matter what cycle you are in.

In strong economies, incomes are rising, property values are increasing, and credit is easy. This is the most dangerous time to over-borrow because everything feels safe. Professional risk management means becoming more conservative when times are good. You borrow less than you could, keep higher reserves, and avoid speculative uses of equity. This ensures you are positioned to survive the next downturn.

In slowing economies, uncertainty increases. Rates may rise, lenders tighten standards, and investments become less predictable. During these periods, HELOCs should be used primarily for strengthening your position, not expanding it.

That might mean paying down high-interest debt, building reserves, or securing fixed-rate financing.

In recessions, cash becomes king. Home values may decline and refinancing becomes harder. The safest HELOC strategy in a recession is to reduce balances and protect liquidity. This is not the time to chase returns. It is the time to make sure your home and cash flow are secure.

In recoveries, opportunities appear. Distressed assets, undervalued properties, and growing demand create fertile ground for careful leverage. Because you preserved your strength during the downturn, you are now able to deploy your HELOC when others cannot.

The key is flexibility. A HELOC is powerful precisely because it is adjustable. When you understand cycles, you stop using equity blindly and start using it strategically.

Practical Example: *Adjusting a HELOC Through a Full Cycle*

Let's look at a homeowner named Rachel. Rachel owns a $600,000 home with a $300,000 mortgage. She has a HELOC and uses $90,000 to invest.

During a strong economy, Rachel's HELOC payment at 9 percent is about $675. Her investments generate $1,200 per month, leaving $525.

When the economy slows and rates rise to 12 percent, her payment increases to $900. Her income drops slightly to $1,100. She now has $200 in margin. She stops borrowing and begins paying down $300 per month.

After one year, her balance drops to $86,400. Her payment falls, restoring margin.

In a recession, her income drops to $900 but her payment is now $864. She uses savings to cover the difference temporarily.

When recovery begins, her balance is lower, her home value stabilizes, and she is ready to invest again.

By adjusting through the cycle, Rachel protects her home and grows wealth over time.

Chapter 14

Passing Wealth Without Passing Risk

One of the most overlooked aspects of home equity planning is what happens after you are gone. A HELOC does not disappear when life changes, it becomes part of your legacy. If it is unmanaged, it can become a burden for your family. If it is structured properly, it becomes a tool that transfers wealth, stability, and opportunity to the next generation. This chapter explains how to use home equity in a way that strengthens your heirs instead of trapping them.

The first principle of legacy planning with a HELOC is clarity. Your family should never be surprised by debt tied to the home. They should know the balance, the purpose of the borrowing, and the plan for paying it off. When information is hidden, stress and mistakes multiply. When it is shared, your family can act intelligently.

The second principle is alignment. Any long-term HELOC balance should be attached to an asset or income stream that outlives you. If you use your HELOC to buy a rental property, a business, or an income-producing investment, your heirs inherit both the debt and the income. That is very different from inheriting debt with no way to service it. The third principle is simplification. As you age, HELOC balances should generally be reduced, not expanded. This lowers complexity for your heirs and increases equity. A highly leveraged home is fragile. A lightly leveraged home is flexible.

The fourth principle is documentation. You should leave behind a written plan that explains what to do with the HELOC, how to manage the assets it funded, and how to unwind everything if needed. This prevents confusion and forced decisions.

The final principle is protection. Proper insurance, trusts, and estate planning tools should be used to make sure the home and the income it produces are shielded from unnecessary taxes, legal battles, or creditor claims.

When you treat your HELOC as part of your legacy plan, it becomes a bridge to generational wealth instead of a risk passed down.

Practical Example: *A HELOC as a Legacy Tool*

Let's look at a homeowner named Thomas. Thomas owns a home worth $800,000 and owes $300,000. He has a $100,000 HELOC balance used to buy a rental property that produces $1,500 per month.

At 9 percent, his HELOC payment is about $750, leaving $750

in profit. Thomas uses $400 to pay down the HELOC and $350 to support his family.

After five years, Thomas has paid down $24,000 of principal. His balance is now $76,000.

When Thomas passes away, his family inherits a home with $300,000 of mortgage and $76,000 of HELOC, but also a rental property generating $1,500 per month. That income easily covers the $600 remaining HELOC payment and continues to produce cash flow.

Because Thomas structured his HELOC with income and documentation, his family inherits wealth, not stress.

Chapter 15

The Lifetime Home Equity Playbook

The final stage of mastering HELOC risk management is turning everything you have learned into a lifetime strategy. Your home equity is not a one-time opportunity, it is a renewable financial resource that can support you through every phase of life if it is managed correctly. This chapter shows how to use HELOCs not as short-term fixes, but as a long-term wealth engine that adapts as you grow, earn, invest, and eventually retire.

In your early years of homeownership, your primary goal is stability. Your income may still be growing, your savings may be limited, and your equity is just beginning to build. During this phase, HELOC use should be conservative. The focus should be on eliminating high-interest debt, building emergency reserves, and possibly funding small, safe investments that improve cash flow. The goal is not to maximize leverage, but to strengthen your financial foundation.

As you move into your peak earning years, your HELOC becomes a powerful accelerator. Your income is higher, your equity has grown, and your risk tolerance is stronger. This is when you can use home equity to acquire rental properties, fund businesses, or invest in assets that produce long-term income. Because you have already built reserves and discipline, this leverage works for you instead of against you.

Later in life, your focus shifts again. The goal becomes preservation and simplicity. HELOC balances should gradually be reduced, not expanded. Income from the assets you built should replace the need for borrowing. Your home becomes a base of security instead of a source of leverage. This ensures peace of mind and protects your family.

The lifetime playbook is about timing. You do not use your HELOC the same way at 35 as you do at 55 or 75. You adapt. What never changes is your commitment to cash flow, reserves, low loan-to-value, and clear exit strategies.

By following this playbook, your home becomes a financial ally for your entire life. It supports growth when you need it and stability when you want it.

Practical Example: *A Lifetime of Safe Leverage*

Let's look at a homeowner named Daniel. Daniel buys his first home at 35 for $400,000 with a $320,000 mortgage. He has $80,000 in equity.

At 40, his home is worth $500,000 and he owes $280,000. He opens a HELOC and uses $50,000 to pay off credit cards and start a small business. His HELOC payment is about $375 per month. The business generates $1,000 per month, leaving $625.

By 50, Daniel's home is worth $650,000 and his total debt is $300,000. His equity is $350,000. He uses another $80,000 to buy a rental that generates $1,400 per month. His total HELOC payment becomes about $975, but his income increases by $1,400.

By 60, Daniel has paid down much of his HELOC and his rental and business produce enough income to cover his living expenses. His home is mostly debt-free.

By following the lifetime playbook, Daniel used his home to build wealth without ever risking losing it.

Final Thoughts

Home equity is one of the most powerful financial tools ever placed into the hands of ordinary people, yet it is also one of the most misunderstood. Throughout this book you have learned that HELOCs are neither good nor bad by themselves. They are instruments. In the hands of someone who understands risk, they become engines of opportunity. In the hands of someone who ignores structure, they become silent threats. The difference is not luck. The difference is discipline, planning, and respect for the math.

What separates professionals from consumers is not access to capital, it is how they manage it. Banks, hedge funds, and real estate firms survive for generations because they never allow a single decision to put the entire enterprise at risk. They think in systems, buffers, and exit strategies. By the time you reach the end of this book, you now think the same way about your home equity. You no longer see a HELOC as free money or easy cash. You see it as a financial lever that must be balanced by cash flow, equity, liquidity, and exits.

The greatest danger of leverage is not that it exists, but that it feels invisible when it is working. When payments are affordable and investments are performing, it is tempting to push harder, borrow more, and assume tomorrow will always look like today. This book was written to protect you from that illusion. Risk management is not about fear. It is about ensuring that no matter what the economy does, no matter what life brings, your home remains a foundation instead of a liability.

By applying what you have learned here, you are no longer dependent on perfect conditions. You know how to stress-test your numbers. You know how to protect your cash flow. You know how to maintain reserves. You know how to build exits. Most importantly, you know how to recognize when it is time to slow down or step back. These are the skills that keep families safe and allow wealth to grow steadily instead of explosively and dangerously.

Your home is more than where you live. It is a financial asset that, when managed correctly, can support businesses, investments, education, and freedom. But unlike other assets, it also carries emotional weight. It is where your family sleeps. It is where memories are made. That is why it deserves a higher standard of care than any other financial tool. HELOC risk management is not about squeezing every dollar of value out of your house. It is about using just enough leverage to improve your life while protecting everything that matters. The future will always bring change. Interest rates will rise and fall.

Markets will cycle. Opportunities will come and go. With the framework you now have, you do not need to predict the future to be safe in it. You have a system that adapts. You have rules that protect you. You have a plan for growth and a plan for retreat. That is what financial confidence really is.

If you carry one idea forward from this book, let it be this: leverage is only dangerous when it is unmanaged. When it is structured, monitored, and backed by real cash flow, it becomes one of the most reliable ways to build long-term wealth. Your HELOC is not something to fear. It is something to respect and master.

The goal is not to be the biggest borrower. The goal is to be the longest-lasting investor. When you protect your home, you protect your future.

How to Get a Personalized HELOC Review

If you found *HELOC Fundamentals: How Home Equity Lines of Credit Really Work — and How to Use Them Safely* helpful, you may want to see how these concepts apply to your own home, credit profile, and financial goals.

Every homeowner's situation is unique. Home value, mortgage balance, credit history, income type, and state-specific lending rules all affect how much equity you can access, what type of HELOC you may qualify for, and what terms may be available. The examples in this book are designed to teach how HELOCs work — but your real options can only be determined by reviewing your actual numbers.

If you would like a **no-obligation Home Equity Line of Credit review**, you can request one here:

Website:https://www.nodocsheloc.com

Email:info@FinibiMortgage.com

A licensed mortgage broker will review your information and explain what HELOC and home equity options may be available to you based on your specific situation.

No cost. No pressure. No obligation.

Joseph G. Correa

About the Author

Joseph G. Correa is a licensed mortgage broker and the founder of Finibi Mortgage, a Florida-based brokerage specializing in home equity, real estate investment financing, and alternative lending strategies for homeowners, business owners, and investors. With more than two decades of experience in mortgage lending, underwriting, and financial structuring, Joseph has helped thousands of borrowers access capital using intelligent, low-risk leverage rather than high-interest consumer debt.

Unlike traditional loan officers who focus only on closing transactions, Joseph's approach is rooted in long-term financial strategy. He believes that mortgages, HELOCs, and credit lines should be used as tools for building wealth, protecting cash flow, and creating financial resilience — not as traps that keep families locked into decades of unnecessary interest payments. This philosophy has made him a trusted advisor for entrepreneurs, real estate investors, and self-employed borrowers who need flexible, modern financing solutions that banks often fail to provide.

Joseph is widely known for his expertise in home equity lines of credit, no-documentation and bank-statement loan programs, investor financing, and creative equity-based strategies such as debt-elimination systems and capital recycling. His ability to translate complex lending rules into simple, actionable guidance has helped homeowners turn idle equity into productive capital for investments, businesses, and passive income.

Through his education platform, Finibi Academy, Joseph has trained tens of thousands of students worldwide in credit, mortgage strategy, real estate financing, and financial independence. His courses and books are used by first-time homeowners, seasoned investors, and financial professionals seeking a clearer, more honest understanding of how modern lending really works.

Joseph created *The Home Equity Wealth Series* to give everyday homeowners the same financial knowledge that banks, hedge funds, and institutional investors use to control capital and minimize risk. His mission is simple: to help people stop guessing, stop fearing debt, and start using smart leverage to build real financial freedom.

When he is not structuring loans or writing, Joseph works with families and investors across the United States to design personalized equity strategies that align with their goals, cash flow, and long-term wealth plans.

The Home Equity Wealth Series Roadmap

The Professional Guide to Using Your Home to Build Financial Freedom

The purpose of *The Home Equity Wealth Series* is to give homeowners the same financial tools and strategies used by banks, investors, and institutions–translated into clear, practical guidance for everyday people. Each book builds on the last, taking you from basic understanding to advanced mastery of how to use home equity safely, intelligently, and profitably across every stage of life.

Book 1 — *HELOC Fundamentals*This book gives you the foundation. You will understand how Home Equity Lines of Credit work, how they are structured, how risk is controlled, and how equity becomes usable capital. The books that follow are designed to help you apply that knowledge to your own situation, your income type, your credit profile, and your long-term financial goals.

Book 2 — *How to Qualify for a HELOC* This book shows you how lenders actually evaluate borrowers. You will learn how credit scores, income, property type, and debt ratios affect approval, limits, and interest rates. You will also learn how to position yourself to qualify for the largest possible credit line at the best possible terms.

Book 3 — *HELOCs for Real Estate Investors* This book focuses on using home equity to buy, rehab, refinance, and scale rental properties. It explains how investors use HELOCs for down payments, renovations, and portfolio growth while keeping cash flow positive and risk controlled.

Book 4 — *Self-Employed HELOC Strategies* Designed for business owners, freelancers, 1099 borrowers, and LLCs, this book explains how bank-statement income, business income, and alternative documentation can be used to qualify for home equity even when traditional tax returns do not reflect true cash flow.

Book 5 — *Credit Mastery for HELOC Approval* This book dives deep into credit strategy. You will learn how utilization, credit mix, and reporting behavior affect HELOC limits and pricing—and how to optimize your credit profile specifically for home equity approval.

Book 6 — *No-Doc & Alternative HELOC Programs* This book covers asset-based HELOCs, no-income-verification options, and non-traditional lending programs for high-net-worth, self-employed, or cash-heavy borrowers who do not fit inside standard underwriting models.

Book 7 — *Using a HELOC to Eliminate Debt* This book teaches how to use home equity to replace high-interest credit cards, personal loans, and auto loans with low-interest revolving credit, allowing borrowers to eliminate debt years faster and save tens of thousands of dollars in interest.

Book 8 — *Using a HELOC to Build Wealth* This book shows how homeowners fund investments, businesses, and passive income streams using HELOCs while maintaining liquidity and controlling risk.

Book 9 — *HELOC Risk Management* This book focuses entirely on safety. You will learn how to structure buffers, cash-flow coverage, rate protection, and leverage limits so your home becomes safer over time—not more vulnerable.

Book 10 — *The Smart Borrower's Home Equity Blueprint* The final book ties everything together into a complete lifetime strategy for using home equity as a personal banking system, investment engine, and financial safety net.

Book 11 — *The Cashflow Accelerator Method*

The Cashflow Accelerator Method is the final transformation stage of *The Home Equity Wealth Series*. While the earlier books teach how to access, qualify for, and safely use home equity, this book teaches how to **weaponize cash flow itself** to permanently eliminate debt and create lasting wealth. Together, these books are designed to turn a single asset—your home—into a lifelong financial advantage. Each volume adds another layer of understanding, allowing you to move from homeowner to capital manager, from borrower to strategist, and from financial stress to long-term stability.

This is not about taking more risk.It is about learning how money really works—and using that knowledge to build financial freedom that lasts.

Educational & Financial Disclaimer

This book is provided for **educational and informational purposes only**. The author and publisher are not engaged in rendering legal, tax, accounting, investment, or financial advice. Although the author is a licensed mortgage broker, the information in this book is intended to provide general education about Home Equity Lines of Credit (HELOCs) and home equity strategy, not personalized financial, legal, or lending advice.

Mortgage programs, underwriting guidelines, interest rates, credit requirements, and home equity products vary by lender, investor, state, and economic conditions, and may change at any time without notice. The examples, calculations, and scenarios presented in this book are hypothetical and are for illustration only. They do not represent guaranteed outcomes or actual loan approvals.

Before making any financial decisions, including applying for a HELOC, refinancing, borrowing against home equity, or using credit for investment or debt repayment, readers should consult with a qualified mortgage professional, financial advisor, tax advisor, or attorney who can evaluate their specific situation.

Risk Disclosure

Borrowing against home equity involves risk. A HELOC is secured by your home, which means failure to make required payments could result in foreclosure or loss of property. This book teaches responsible, conservative, and structured use of home equity, but no financial strategy is risk-free.

Readers are solely responsible for their financial decisions. Neither the author nor the publisher makes any warranties, express or implied, about the accuracy, completeness, or applicability of the information in this book to any individual or situation.

www.ingramcontent.com/pod-product-compliance
Ingram Content Group UK Ltd.
Pitfield, Milton Keynes, MK11 3LW, UK
UKHW020157290926
15471UKWH00005B/919

9 798295 576560